i

Books by Ray Hollenbach

The Impossible Mentor: Finding Courage to Follow Jesus

25 Days of Christmas

One Month of Thanksgiving

50 Forgotten Days

The Man With All The Answers

The Gospel of Matthew

Deeper Grace

Deeper
HOPE

Ray Hollenbach

Published by Lone Valley Publishing,
Campbellsville, KY 42718

Cover photo by Sarah Ward
Used by her kind permission.

For
Madeline
Carraway,
Heath, &
Dexter

Each one a gift of hope.

Acknowledgments

This book is about discovering—and sharing—hope. Each "chapter" is short. I had a rhythm in mind: read, and meditate; study, and understand; receive, and invite others into the conversation.

It began as a Kickstarter project, and would not exist without the nearly 100 supporters who encouraged and pledged their support seven months before the publication date. I owe each one a debt of gratitude that goes far beyond any "reward level" at that site.

I should've expected that writing a book about hope would probably lead me into new territory. I didn't expect the new territory included the death of my mother-in-law, Diana Salmon, a woman I have treasured for more than 30 years. Together my wife, Kim, and I walked into new levels of both grief and hope, and that journey has (I trust) made the book better.

I owe thanks to Pastor Robin McMillan of Queen City Church in Charlotte, NC, who lit the fires of hope for me in a new way. Robin reflected on Hebrews 11:1: "If faith is the substance of our hopes," he said, "then our level of faith cannot rise above the level of our hope." His observation spurred me to action.

Finally, I'm so very grateful to Patrick Steed, who volunteered to proof read the book, and did so under an unreasonably short deadline, and he did it as a gesture of friendship. (Thanks, Patrick.) Still, any errors in the book are entirely my responsibility.

ix

Friday for mourning
Saturday for hope
Sunday for joy

Saturday is the test we fail.

Saturday locks the door.
Dead bolt. Security system. Gun under the pillow.
Every entrance sealed against the grace beyond.

But we are locked in.
What would happen if, on our best day,
We stepped into the danger and saw the beauty?

Table of Contents

"Hope means hoping when things are hopeless, or it is no virtue at all . . . As long as matters are really hopeful, hope is mere flattery or platitude; it is only when everything is hopeless that hope begins to be a strength."

~ G.K. Chesterton

Introduction

Everything that is done in the world is done by hope. ~
Martin Luther

If you and I are going to spend some time together in
this book you need to know one of my dreadful secrets:
I cry at happy endings. All of them: movies, music,
even when someone wins the Grand Prize Showcase
on *The Price Is Right.* This means I cry a lot. And I cry
ugly.

I'm not usually given to outbursts of emotion. I like to
think of myself as a levelheaded, rational sage. I know
that producers of movies and TV shows are capable of
all manner of manipulation to make you forget the
loose ends in the story, to help you forget that the good
guys destroyed six city blocks while fighting the bad
guys, but as long as the narcissistic hero gets the girl
and saves the world, I'm weepy. Roll the credits.

Country music is famous for *sad* songs: let that cowboy
lose his job, his truck, his dog and his girl. Nice try, I
won't cry. Nope. Too bad for you, pardner. But just let
Carrie Underwood sing *Jesus Take the Wheel* and I'm
looking for the tissue while trying not to attract
attention to myself. (Actually, I'm a classic Rock guy to
the core, but if the playlist includes something sappy
like The Monkees' *Daydream Believer,* I'm singing. Out
loud.)

I used to think it was because I'm a sucker for
sentimentality, but I'm convinced there's something

1

deeper going on. The truth is, I'm moved to tears whenever I see hope fulfilled. When hope pays off, I feel the rush. When the hero has risked everything while everyone else has written her off as a fool, I'm with her.

I'd go so far as to say I'm a hope junkie. It's a high like none other. In fact, it comes from *on high*; it's the feeling you can get when Heaven breaks into everyday life. Hope fulfilled is more than simply good news or good fortune. In order to feel the joy of hope fulfilled, we must first have bet the farm on hope. We must have risked something: our reputation, our safety, our sanity.

Before we can hope we must dare to care about something, or someone. An outcome must matter; the ending must mean something. Hope is never simply about happy endings because, like a gambler, we must push our chips in the center of the table and wager our wellbeing. And the chips rarely represent money; more likely what we have wagered is our hearts. There's no sure thing. Before hope can be fulfilled, we must take the great risk of daring to hope. We must become the fools who care.

Perhaps this is the great wager of hope: are we willing to be fools? When we cannot calculate the odds, or when the odds seem remarkably tilted against us, will we dare to hope? In what (or in whom) will we hope? Always in the back of our minds there is a voice that cautions: *Be careful! Don't go too far. Everyone is watching. Why should you be the one who risks failing? You'll look like a fool! You'll get hurt! You'll get hurt again! What happens when you find out it was only wishful thinking?*

This slim book is for you—and also the voice inside you urging caution—because they are one and the same. Come with me and explore the possibilities of hope. (The crying is optional.)

Scary Hope

May your choices reflect your hopes, not your fears. ~
Nelson Mandela

My father had a battery-operated dinosaur. It was a
ludicrous little toy, furry like a bear but it stood upright
like a T Rex, with those tiny front arms. When you
flipped a switch the dinosaur would come alive and
waddle an awkward four steps, stop, then its eyes
would glow a fiery red, like Godzilla's. The little T Rex
arms would rise up and the six-inch beast would make
a mechanical growling sound.

I took my three year-old son to visit his grandfather.
Grandpa put the dinosaur on the floor, flipped the
switch and the bizarre little show began. My son was
fascinated by the mechanical noise and the awkward
side-to-side steps. But when the eyes glowed red and a
little T Rex arms reached up and the growling sound
came forth, tinny and mechanical, my son stepped
back in horror, truly frightened by the toy. But he could
not look away from the dinosaur. He was alternately
attracted to the furry waddling creature and then
repelled by the fiery eyes and the terrible growl. The
two of them, my son and the dinosaur, danced all
afternoon, my son coming dangerously close and then
backing away, the dinosaur waddling after him four
steps at a time.

It went on all afternoon, the alternation of attraction
and fear. The interplay of fascination and anxiety. The
rhythm of attraction and repulsion. The possibilities of
play and the fear of the unknown. And of course my

son is not alone: hope waddles toward us like a ridiculous furry toy.

On the surface hope seems safe enough: a pleasant distraction from the real work of everyday life. It is harmless dreaming or gentle consolation. But underneath the greeting card sentiments about hope lives something stronger, something with substance, something perhaps even dangerous. We are strangely attracted to the possibilities of hope—until its eyes glow red and hope reaches for us with fuzzy reptilian arms. Hope threatens to take possession of us. If we are not careful, hope—real, substantial hope—can consume us. It will pull us into a surreal world and ask us to believe impossible things. So we run, but not too far. Hope draws us back again and somehow we just can't look away.

Or another metaphor: Hope, a Christian virtue that on the surface seems so pleasant and comfortable, is more like an Olympic gymnast: dressed in glittering spandex and bows and all made up with too much eye shadow, and—just when we're tempted to dismiss the glam as a lightweight harmless occupation, hope steps on to the competitive floor and shows us the possibilities of life: leaping, twisting, somersaulting and defying gravity. The challenge of this athletic, gymnastic hope is that it demonstrates the potential of life lived to the full. We can all defy gravity if we dare to hope, and learn from hope how to master our bodies and our minds. Hopeful people leap, twist, and somersault. Hope-filled people are strong and flexible. Hope-filled people are not earth-bound: they fly.

And here is their secret: when the furry dinosaur turns a fearful red and reaches for them, they allow themselves to be captured by hope. That's how it starts. Will we

6

allow ourselves to see past the harmless charm of a domesticated hope and be carried away by the real thing?

The Beauty of Hope

Hope inspires the good to reveal itself.
~ Emily Dickinson

The beauty of hope is that although we have been cut and wounded time and again by life, the blade of despair has not reached our hearts. But there is danger still: the blade is poisoned with cynicism, and so our blood has become infected. Hope is the antidote to the poison.

The beauty of hope shows itself as innocence in the face of evidence to the contrary. Hope is the connection to the better angels of our nature. Hope is bowed by neither reasoning nor the evening news. Hope is the memory of a timeless garden where humanity lived as one with nature and nature's God. Hope is memory without words, memory without event; hope is the witness of our souls.

Hope is a young girl opening a cedar chest and storing away the accessories of a future life. She is imagining the days and decades ahead, when she will share life with a husband yet unmet. She has no clear idea of what marriage is like; she has no concept of the challenges two sinful people face when they join their lives together. Her view of marriage is filled with the stuff of romance novels and fairy tales—and yet into the Hope Chest she places items both practical and inspirational. Her hope chest holds a KitchenAid mixer and embroidered Bible verses, dishes and napkins and

9

baby clothes. Who knows whether they will be used? The hope chest, silent and still in the corner of her bedroom, is the promise a new kind of life. "Quaint," you say. "Beautiful," I reply.

The beauty of hope is in the risk. Before hope can be fulfilled we must take the great risk of daring to hope. The cynic thinks he knows better, but what if he only knows worse? Why shouldn't a young girl hope for an idyllic marriage? Or a young woman hope for children? Or a mother hope for a long and healthy life for her child? Hope is an expression of love, perhaps even a love we ourselves know nothing about. Hope leans into the future and strengthens us to pursue it in practical ways.

Hope cross-examines us when the eyewitness account of our own experience might actually be false testimony. We know what we saw—or at least we think we do—until we sit in the dock and face hard questions. Hope is the defense attorney who leads us to reconsider our version of events. Perhaps our past has colored our view of the future. Perhaps we can't even remember the past the way it really was. Hope comes along and challenges our conclusions because the "school of hard knocks" has actually given us a concussion. Perhaps we have lived in the fog of bitterness and doubt. What if the defense attorney is trying to set us free? Anne Lamott suggests this very thing when she says, "This is who I think we are supposed to be, people who help call forth human beings from deep inside hopelessness."

The beauty of hope is not limited to the young. The New York Times recently covered the wedding of a 98 year-old woman to a 94 year-old man. They met at the gym. "I asked him to marry me," said Gertrude

Mokotoff, the *older woman.* "I was tired of chasing after him."

Hope shows itself among the wrinkles and arthritic joints and the slow-motion pace of the aged: not only at the gym, but in the halls of retirement homes, where old people have been stowed away for safe keeping. There, in a company of the no-longer-needed, blue-hairs and greybeards create not-so-quiet communities that are tucked away from sight of others. That's the way it is with hope: it thrives in out of the way places.

The beauty of hope is not the beauty of fashion magazines or the Hollywood red carpet. One lesson we all learn too quickly is the fading nature of physical beauty. To find true beauty we must look elsewhere. Physical beauty should be appreciated and perhaps even celebrated, but it should not be trusted. The beauty of hope is attractive only to those who know the value of love and faith, those who understand that most everything in this world is passing away and not many things will survive from this age into the age to come. Only three things will remain untouched from this age into the next: faith, hope, and love. Hope hangs out in the company of faith and love. Hope is an abiding thing; it will outlast this world.

Unseen Hope

Though you lose all hope, there is still hope, and it
loves to surprise. ~ Robert Brault

"Hope that is seen is not hope," says the Apostle Paul.

Hope takes us into the unseen; hope lures us into a
supernatural future. Frederick Buechner may not have
had it completely right when he said, "This is your life:
beautiful and terrible things will happen." Perhaps he
should've said, "Here are your hopes: beautiful and
terrible things will happen."

"The unseen" can mean many things. The unseen
could mean *the future*, which we cannot see. But it can
mean more something more. The unseen can mean
that we simply lack the ability to see something our
eyes are incapable of seeing, like the wind. We might
see the results of the wind, as when the grass moves
ever so gently as the air moves it like a brush. But there
is more. Ask any physicist about the unseen. The
scientist will tell you that the world is made up of
empty space: the distance between the nucleus and the
electrons. Yet in that tiny space mysterious forces
dance about, exerting their influence on both the
center and the edges. The same is true in the
macrocosm of space: our vast universe is seemingly
filled with—nothing! Yet in that nothing teem primal
forces that set the galaxy spinning and the universe
expanding, the edges of which we only think we have
discovered.

When you think of the future, what emotions rise up in you? For some people the future means a continuation of the past, only more so. What will be is largely determined by what has been. There is certain logic to this approach: in some ways our present lives represent the results of past choices. For others the future means the possibility of change, the chance to chart a new course or establish a new reality. This, too, makes sense. Fresh choices lead to new horizons. It's a wonder there's future at all—who says the next moment must come?

There is one more way to consider this unseen future. Beyond our legacy of the past or our ability to choose lies a supernatural future. The future could include God's supernatural dabbling in our lives, things literally beyond our imagination:

> "What no eye has seen,
>   what no ear has heard,
> and what no human mind has conceived,
>   the things God has prepared for those who
> love him" (1 Corinthians 2:9)

The little voice inside my own head raises an objection: *maybe this is simply the religious version of wishful thinking, a kind of Christian optimism.* This is the voice of my humanity, the part of me that believes self-preservation is the highest good, even at he expense of others—whatever it takes to keep me alive and on top. Or maybe it's the intersection of hope and faith. "For we walk by faith, not by sight," the Apostle Paul reminds us elsewhere. Those who insist on walking by sight forfeit the possibilities of hope, supernatural hope, good and perfect gifts waiting to be received.

14

Godly hope changes our perspective: it expands our horizon from a handful of decades into the span of eternity. Hope is a comfort beyond time.

It turns out that unseen hope is the only kind of hope there is. The God of all hope (another phrase from Paul) is not seen with our eyes, nor would he be worth worshipping if we could see him. And really—why would it be anything other than this? It should come as no surprise that in order to worship the unseen God requires of us hope in the unseen.

Reflection #1

Have you ever stared off into space, not really focused on anything? Me too. In my experience such a gaze comes with another lack of focus: I find that my thoughts stop as well. My brain goes silent at the same time my vision goes blurred. (I know what you're thinking: *maybe he's had a stroke!*)

Perhaps there is a physiological explanation for this kind of pause. I dunno. But there's definitely a spiritual one. Consider this passage from the Apostle Paul:

> *We fix our eyes not on what is seen, but on what is unseen, since what is seen is temporary, but what is unseen is eternal. (2 Corinthians 4:16-18)*

How do we do this? How do we *focus* on what we cannot *see?*

Here is an exercise in meditation: The way toward hope, the discipline of hope, is to patiently discard every thought, every idea *we* can generate about our life or situation, and to gaze upon the unseen, to listen to the unspoken. In short: to simply be with Him.

Try this sometime: in a quiet place and in an unhurried way, set aside your ability to reason or even to verbalize your thoughts. Let your eyes and mind stare into Heaven's space. You needn't fear: if we ask for the Holy Spirit's presence we can be sure the Spirit will meet us. Some of our most hope-filled moments will come not from what is seen, thought, or heard, but from what is neither seen nor heard.

Hope and Promise

"By hope we lay hands on the substance of
what we believe and by hope we possess the
promise of God's love." ~ Thomas Merton

The Father reaches out to us through his great and
precious promises. Hope encourages us to reach
toward him with both hands, ready to grasp his love.

I hear God's promise, perhaps through reading the
scripture or listening in prayer. The promise requires
something of me: to believe, to hope. When I respond
with hope the promise comes alive in me, it no longer
resides in a book or as an idea, it becomes a living
thing.

It's too easy to reduce the words of God to principles
and precepts, as if the Father is the Great Theology
Lecturer in the Sky. But no: he is personal, intimate,
and close. No amount of study can achieve this
intimacy. Intellectuals value learning; the desperate
value hope. God's promises are not grandiose
proclamations from a mountaintop; they are love-
words whispered in my ear—secrets known only to
him and me. His promises are not the stuff of contracts
and agreements that lawyers can parse and accountants
measure; they are bread and wine that sustain my body
and lift my spirit.

Each promise from God is personal, even if it is given
to many people. Others might hear the very same

19

words and stand unmoved or evaluate the promise with a critical eye. *Trusting this promise is a high-risk strategy,* they judge. *There's no guarantee of success; the odds are against this plan.* But hope is not a strategy: it is birthed when the words of loving parent are received and treasured by a trusting child. We cannot really believe the promises of God until we take the dangerous step of trusting him.

The Apostle Peter understood the dynamic power released in us when place our hope in the promises of God. "Because of his glory and excellence," he writes in the first chapter of II Peter , "he has given us great and precious promises. These are the promises that enable you to share his divine nature and escape the world's corruption caused by human desires." Hope leads us toward the divine nature and leads us away from the corrupting power of our own desires apart from his promises. It's not that desire itself is bad; it's that the promises of God are the proper object of desire. Our desires, comfort, ease, security, wealth, and control actually corrupt our souls. Human desires apart from God's promises will wear us down and break us apart—that's what corruption is. But desire, when pointed toward God's promises, become a life-giving tree, rooted deep within us. "Hope deferred makes the heart sick," say the Proverbs, "But desire fulfilled is a tree of life." When our hope is in anything other than the promises of God, we will find ourselves heartsick.

There is a modern word for this sickness of the heart: cynicism. Cynicism is an infection that poisons the everyday blessings of life and multiplies the everyday problems of life. Despair is not the opposite of hope: cynicism is. Cynicism is anti-trust; it is the whispered voice of caution that flows from the self, a self

20

separated from the love of God. It is the illness of our age, presented to us as the wisdom of the worldly-wise, self-preservation masquerading as intelligence.

Why is cynicism regarded as a useful tool for coping with life but hope is written off as wishful thinking? Hope is the more powerful force for change. Let others label hope as risky: the real risk is to live our lives as if God does not exist. The day will come when the scoffers and cynics will stand amazed that the small and the foolish were right all along: hope is the way forward.

Speaking Hope

Where there's hope, there's life. It fills us with fresh
courage and makes us strong again. ~ Anne Frank

Hope becomes effective in our lives when we speak it
out loud. Hope dies in us when we can no longer talk
about it. It takes faith to speak up, but faith has nothing
to say until it is informed by hope. Faith and hope are
fellow travelers.

The Father whispers his promises to us. We hear him
from deep in our innermost place. But promises are not
secrets; some things should be declared. Jesus
instructed us, "What I tell you in the dark, speak in the
daylight; what is whispered in your ear, proclaim from
the roofs." (Matthew 10:27) This means putting our
hopes on display long before they are fulfilled. This
means taking the risk of sharing with others the hopes
God has put into our hearts. Too often we have limited
our testimony to what has happened in the past. Our
full testimony must include our hope for the future.

But it's dangerous. What if we are wrong? What if we
didn't hear God at all and it was just wishful thinking?
Wouldn't it be better to write our hopes down in a
journal and hide them away until after they are
fulfilled?

The risk of speaking—and *pursuing*—our hope might
cause us to keep the secrets of God's promises as a
private dream. The counsel of safety says its better to
leave our hopes tucked away in our hearts, unspoken
and safe from the advice of others who might question

whether God has really spoken. Temptation begins with the question, "Did God say . . .?" It might end with the suggestion to lower our sights, or to keep things on the down-low until we are sure of the result. But hope asks the opposite of us: to be the fools who speak up. Dreams are not really dreams unless we have dared to share them with others. And joy is multiplied when we give voice to those promises our heart has heard. The courage to hope includes the courage to speak and move and act. Hope is born in secret but flourishes in the light. The way to keep hope alive is to fill your lungs and breathe out words of faith.

Can you think of people who've done this? People who refuse to silence their hopes? Certainly there are great figures in history, people like Dr. Martin Luther King, Jr., Winston Churchill, or Mother Teresa—a woman who dared to remind presidents and popes that the image of God could be found on the streets of the poorest people. Nor is the voice of hope found only on the tongues of the famous: hope is the common property of all God's children, and the sound of hope should amplify all our words. But we, the everyday people of God, too often silence words of hope because we do not want to appear foolish or trite. We are sometimes fooled into thinking that expressing our hope clearly amounts to pushing our opinions on others.

In fact, this is how hope dies: when we dare not speak its name. When we hide the God-given light of hope under a bushel, depriving it the air it so desperately needs, it flickers and dies, unseen, unheard, and unnoticed by others until we ourselves utter it no more. But hope is the birthright of all who are created in God's image, and we are the bearers of hope.

Hope and Grief

There is more hope in honest brokenness than in the pretense of false wholeness.

~ Jamie Arpin-Ricci

Let me say this up front: I'm no expert on grief, unless you count my ability to grieve in all manner of unhealthy ways, like avoidance or eating. But there's no getting around a conversation about the relationship between hope and grief. It is a conversation we have all had, or will have. How can you experience deeper hope apart from real grief?

While I was writing this book our family suffered the loss of our matriarch, my mother-in-law (her name was Diana—it feels so stilted to use her title). Our family has lived together in close-knit love. We live on what used to be a farm, and over the years the acres have been divided among the family members. We built houses within sight of one another, live within walking distance. Sundays, almost without fail, we gathered in Diana's kitchen and ate together, sharing the events of our lives both small and big. We spent long, lazy afternoons sitting on the front porch without any agenda other than being together. This was the family rhythm for decades. Then, without much warning, Diana fell sick and died over the span of just a few months.

So here's the sum total of what I know about grief: it's real, it's deep, and it's a part of life. The prophet Isaiah described Jesus as a man "acquainted with grief." Jesus stood at the tomb of his friend Lazarus and wept—even as he knew he was about to raise Lazarus back to life.

The apostle Paul, using some of his most pastoral language, talked about grief to his friends in Thessalonica:

> But we do not want you to be uninformed, brothers and sisters, about those who have died, so that you may not grieve as others do who have no hope. For since we believe that Jesus died and rose again, even so, through Jesus, God will bring with him those who have died. (1 Thessalonians 4:13-14)

Grieving is a part of living together, and hope does not eliminate grief—but it does change the nature of grief. Who is qualified, really, to lecture about hope in the face of death? Not me: I won't tell you anything new or insightful. But I have found myself leaning on Paul's words because they allow me to live between the tension of two worlds: we do not grieve like those who have no hope, but we do grieve—and we have hope. All I can tell you is it's true.

Here's the one thing that changed for us in the process. When Diana died our family used all the phrases you'd expect to hear. No one had any deep revelations about God, or life, or the resurrection. Before her death I used to shake my heart at those unoriginal words you hear repeated in funeral homes. We simply added our voice to the chorus of those who had said them before, but the words were different because now they were about Diana.

And this happened: for the first time in my life the words from Hebrews chapter 12 became more than

28

doctrine, they became personal. Do you remember them?

"*Therefore, since we are surrounded by so great a cloud of witnesses, let us also lay aside every weight and the sin that clings so closely, and let us run with perseverance the race that is set before us . . .*"

I've always thought the cloud of witnesses referred to those exceptional saints listed in the previous chapter. Yet after 32 years of relationship with Diana, I had come to see *her* as an exceptional hero of faith, even though few people knew her name or her story. But *I* did. And now *I knew someone* in that cloud, a cloud of witnesses who are watching us, urging us onward because without us their lives are somehow not complete. They need us to remain faithful and true, and they are watching. Is it too strange to say that Diana's passing makes me want to be a better person? Only through her death have I begun to draw comfort from the idea that others are looking on. Her passing gives me hope that the silly events of my days can be filled with hope and that my life matters enough that someone wants to look on, urging me to follow Jesus more closely, love my family more fully, and finish that portion of the race that is for me to run.

So I grieve—and run—full of hope.

The Reservoir of Hope

Hope is the thing with feathers that perches in the soul, and sings the tunes without the words, and never stops at all. ~ Emily Dickinson

Somewhere in the heavens a giant reservoir holds an ingredient essential to life: hope. Heaven is saturated with hope; it does not stay in the skies, it rains upon us.

In the 21st century hope is simply the poetic version of wishful thinking. These days hope is the stuff of dreams: it's as thin as the air. It's the currency of desperation. In the modern world hope is a counterfeit traded by losers. The simple word hope has come to mean something unsure and doubtful. Everyone hopes for the best, but prepares for the worst. When we talk about hope in everyday language we are really talking about our insecurities: who knows how things will really work out?

But last night I read these amazing words: "*the faith and love that spring from hope that is stored up for you in heaven.*" (Colossians 1:5) The Apostle Paul was writing to a community of believers he had never met. He had heard of their faith in Jesus. He had heard of their love for one another. Paul knew immediately that these people had tapped into an eternal source capable of funding such faith and love. They had tapped into hope.

This is a revelation: in heaven, where every need is met and there's no more crying or sorrow, hope remains. Paul describes it as the stockpile of heaven, ready to

31

energize faith and love in the here and now. Why would we love another person if there were no hope for them? Why would we have faith the promises of God unless there is evidence that these promises are sure?

The "hope of heaven" is not a destination; it's a resource. The hope of Heaven is a resource available to us now. Even in the valley of despair, a door of hope remains open, because heaven is open to us now. Hope is our anchor, but instead of casting it into the depths of the seas, we anchor our hope in heaven— that place where God's Kingdom is manifested full. The firm place for the anchor of our souls is not in the hard cold earth, but in the firmament of Heaven. Only God's realm holds us steady

Hope is the rebirth of divine certainty: through hope we see Jesus, the high king of heaven. Food, water, shelter, fame, money and sex are only the illusions of necessity. Hope is the true necessity of life.

The Biblical notion of hope is the opposite of uncertainty. It's a word filled with expectation: expectation of God's powerful intervention. The word hope describes the in-breaking of joy. When the Spirit of God speaks of hope, the word means "confident expectation." It's a lifeline from heaven. It is an overflowing word, intended to be contagious, changing lives and cultures. It's worth saying again: hope is an abiding thing. Godly hope is the rebirth of divine certainty in us, and it does not disappoint

We could spend the next decade plumbing the depths of Biblical hope. We could explore the pathways of hope until we draw our final breath, only to discover that the half has not been told. Here are just a few examples:

- **Hebrews** describes hope as an anchor, thrown—not into the sea—but into the heavens. The preacher of that message suggests hope should spur us to diligence, not out of desperation but rather confidence.
- **Hosea** discovered the "gateway of hope" in the "valley of Trouble."
- **The Psalms** reveal that hope is the antidote for depression and turmoil. Not wishful thinking or a positive mental attitude, but instead drinking deep from springs of hope the way a deer searches for streams of water.
- In **Romans**, the Apostle Paul promised us that hope does not disappoint. Hope is the conduit through which God's love pours into our hearts.

I'm beginning to re-tool my vocabulary, and more importantly my heart. What has God said? What has he promised? I will lash myself to his revelation, because *hope abides*. Our ability to give thanks from the heart depends upon hope: the hope of God's goodness and the hope of his constant presence. The greatest of these may be love, but faith and hope are love's fellow travelers. I suspect there's room for you in the traveling party.

The Who of Hope

Hope sees the invisible, feels the intangible and
achieves the impossible. ~ Helen Keller

The wisest people are not those with all the answers.
Wisdom teaches us to ask the right questions. Asking
the right question leads to the right answer, and the
right answer is always a person—never a reason.
Among the educated, the privileged, or the elite the
right question seems to be *Why*? But among the
humble, the lowly, or the disciple, asking the right
question is the journey from *Why* to *Who*?

Not only are we a people of unclean lips, we have
become a people of prideful questions. On the lips of
the childlike, *Why* is a question of wonder and awe; on
the lips of a grown-up, *Why* becomes a demand for
accountability. *Why* summons those we hold
responsible before the court of our understanding. And
the bigger the issue, it is always God who is called into
question:

Why did God make this happen?

Why didn't God intervene?

Why did God give this illness or take my loved one?

We foolishly believe that if we can understand the
reasons behind an event, we will be equipped to cope

with it. Yet it turns out that *Why* never brings comfort. Cold is the comfort and hollow the explanations of people who deal in Why-answers. We ask, *Why* did this have to happen—and even if we could actually receive a full accounting—it brings no comfort.

Asking *Who* brings the Comforter near. *Why* demands an answer; *Who* seeks a comforter. *Why* deals in theories, ideas and concepts; *Who* leads us to a Person.

Even in the middle of Apostle Paul's most theological letter, filled with theology, explanations, and reasoning we see the importance of *Who*. When he despaired of his wretchedness he cried out "Who will deliver me?" (Romans 7:24)

Who can I turn to?

Who will deliver me?

Who will walk with me?

Deeper still, the question of *Who* always leads us to look beyond ourselves. After we have turned toward the Comforter, the Spirit gently urges us to become the presence of *Who* for others:

> *"Praise be to the God and Father of our Lord Jesus Christ, the Father of compassion and the God of all comfort, who comforts us in all our troubles, so that we can comfort those in any trouble with the comfort we ourselves receive from God." (2 Corinthians 1:3-4)*

Notice the source of our comfort. Our own understanding is over-rated. The comfort is in the Comforter, not in the explanation. This is the heart of ministry, because it's the heart of God, the one who simply promises, "I am with you, always." This is our hope.

Hope In A One-Room Studio Apartment

Hope has two beautiful daughters. Their names are anger and courage; anger at the way things are, and courage to see that they do not remain the way they are. ~ St. Augustine

Hope, promise, and expectation live in the most unlikely places. The birth narrative in Luke's gospel is peopled with unknowns—unknowns who possessed a rich history with God and whose stories are preserved for our instruction. Simeon is just such an example. He was an individual on the margins, unnoticed in his day but preserved for us in the scripture as an example of how to walk with God.

Just after the birth of their child, Mary and Joseph took Jesus to the Temple in Jerusalem. The Temple was a massive complex of buildings, a religious marketplace at the center of Jewish life. The young couple expected anonymity in the crush of humanity flowing in and out of the Temple, but instead they encountered a man who had patiently waited to see the hope of Israel fulfilled before he died:

> Now there was a man in Jerusalem called Simeon, who was righteous and devout. He was waiting for the consolation of Israel, and the Holy Spirit was upon him. It had been revealed to him by the Holy Spirit that he would not die before he had seen the Lord's Christ. Moved by the Spirit, he went

into the temple courts. When the parents brought in the child Jesus to do for him what the custom of the Law required, Simeon took him in his arms and praised God, saying:

"Sovereign Lord, as you have promised,you now dismiss your servant in peace.For my eyes have seen your salvation,which you have prepared in the sight of all people, a light for revelation to the Gentiles and for glory to your people Israel. (Luke 2: 25 – 32)

Simeon's actions and words are recorded for us not as a matter of historical curiosity, but rather to demonstrate how we can enter into God's purpose in our day as well. Simeon had a dynamic relationship with the Holy Spirit. In just three verses the work of the Spirit is highlighted three times, and each mention points to a distinct aspect of the Spirit's work in Simeon's life:

- First the scripture says simply, "the Holy Spirit was upon him." (v25) Simeon's life was characterized by the presence of the Spirit in an abiding way: to know Simeon, to talk with him, was to taste something of the Holy Spirit. Perhaps you have met people like him. Their lives are permeated with the presence of the Holy Spirit. They radiate the attributes of Godly character, sometimes known as "the fruit of the Spirit." In Simeon's case other people may not have been able to define the source of his distinctive character, but they undoubtedly sensed the difference.

- Second, the Holy Spirit had spoken to Simeon personally that "he would not die until he had seen the Lord's Christ." (v26) This is significant because no amount of study in the Old Testament could lead anyone to such a promise. It was personal. That means Simeon had trained not only his intellect but also his spirit to receive from God. Simeon combined both the ability to hear and the faith to hold on to what he heard. Can you imagine the raised eyebrows he would have encountered if he chose to share such a personal promise from God? Yet the promise was true because the scriptures assure us so.

- Third, Simeon followed the leading of the Holy Spirit in practical ways. He was "moved by the Holy Spirit" on a particular day to be at a particular place at a particular time (v27). Perhaps Simeon was consciously aware of the Spirit's direction, or perhaps it was something less defined. But whatever level of awareness Simeon possessed it was sufficient to put him in the right place at the right time. Dallas Willard has observed that God's leading isn't always some explicit command. In fact, we may not be able to separate our thoughts from his— until after the fact, when we realize God was leading and guiding toward a particular moment. Although we do not know Simeon's age at the time of the encounter with Jesus, the text leads us to believe he was a man advanced in years. His interaction with the Holy Spirit that day was not some robotic control. It was the result of years of heartfelt seeking and cooperation with the still small voice so characteristic of God's ways.

Simeon's relationship with the Holy Spirit placed him before the baby Jesus. Simeon's response to the moment is instructive as well:

He knew his moment had come. When Simeon declares, "dismiss your servant in peace," (v29) he is not waxing poetic. He welcomes death because he has experienced the faithfulness of God. He has witnessed the promise of God to Abraham, to Israel, and to himself. He has seen the hope of Israel.

Simeon saw what others did not. He declared, "My eyes have seen your salvation, which you have prepared in the sight of all people" (vs 30-31) It was business as usual at the Temple that day. Priests, rabbis, and religious sorts of all kinds walked right past the King of Glory. Simeon saw a baby and witnessed the consolation of Israel. Here's a difficult question: will I be held accountable for what the Father tried to show me, but I was unable to see?

Finally, *Simeon understood that God's purposes stretch beyond Israel to the entire world.* There, in the shadow of the Temple, Simeon bore witness to the hope of the Gentiles. Most of the Temple was off-limits to women and pagans. But standing before Mary, and attracting the attention of a widow named Anna, Simeon declared that the court of the Gentiles now housed the presence of God. The God of Abraham had fulfilled a promise to bless the entire world. In our day, even among believers, we are tempted to think that God is at work on behalf of the few, when in fact his purposes include the many.

The Life Cycle of Hope

"Patience is not circumstance-enforced passivity. Patience is the practical application of hope." ~ Rebecca Dark

The face of hope changes with age and experience. For some, life increases in wonder and possibilities; for others life is a slow, sure, shutting down. Hope is present at every stage of life. The vital question is whether we have eyes to see the hope that is always before us.

We learn and grow in hope. For a dozen years the first day of school is met with crazy hope. Each fall my Facebook feed is filled with pictures of kids in new outfits, backpacks fresh and new, taken by proud parents as their children begin again the process of discovery. Sure, the little darlings are cute, but what's more interesting to me is the parents who line up the kids and post the pictures, because on the first day of school even the parents buy into the possibilities of hope.

There is hope at graduation, where we take a deep breath and throw those ridiculous hats in the air and shout in victory. Isn't it interesting that a ceremony designed to celebrate the *end* of something is named "commencement"? Here lives ridiculous hope, stoked by fires of adolescent hormones and ignorance, but it is hope nonetheless—exactly what we need to get us through the outrageous fortunes of our first decade as adults.

Hope is a guest at every wedding, where we see joy in the moment and quixotic hope of the days to come. What's fascinating about a wedding is the reception: watch the faces of groomsmen and bridesmaids scanning the room, looking for their ideal match. You'll see middle-aged men and women, reminded of their own success or failure in relationships. And is there anything more joyful than watching the grandparents dance, celebrating not only the new marriage of the day but also the 50 years of hope fulfilled in their own lives?

The young parent working two jobs might be bent over by the responsibilities of life and the harsh reality that so few people care about the needs of others, but each mother or father is fueled by the hope that fidelity and hard work create the slow progress capable of making a difference for both parent and child. Even in our toil, we hope.

Hope is the person who begins saving for retirement—at age 59. Hope is the woman who learns a new language, while seated in the wheelchair of a retirement home. And, of course, there's hope at the grave: observe the family gathered once more, this time in grief, and you'll see there are some people who are convinced there is yet more, something further up and further in.

My father-in-law enjoys his fireplace. He's a master fire-maker. He can start a fire in November and that same fire will burn until March. While the morning coffee is brewing he kneels at the fireplace and stirs the ashes, because he knows that under the ashes of last night's fire are the embers of morning. Those embers are enough to ignite the new fire of the new day. Hope is like the embers of the hearth: the glowing coals that can bring dry wood to life. He also knows that someone must tend the flame: if we lose hope, the fire dies away completely.

Reflection #2

"For whoever is joined with all the living, there is hope; Surely a live dog is better than a dead lion." ~ Ecclesiastes 9:4

How can you tell if you are losing hope? Here is a brief inventory of how we throw our hopes overboard:

- We begin looking for the exits. The effect of losing hope is to begin to look for plan B. Or plan C—or as many letters as it takes to "protect yourself."

  pathways vs. escape routes

- When hope erodes, so do our relationships. We begin to avoid the very people who believe in us most and have the highest hopes for us.

- The silence descends. Despair is born of silence. It gags the expression of our hope. We begin to believe "if I don't say it, if I no longer give voice to my hope, I no longer am faced with the choice to trust in the God of hope." The silence extends to our fears as well: we are afraid to talk about our own fears. In silence, we avoid both hope and fear.

  prayers are rote

This reflection is an exercise in courage. Take a deep breath; then take inventory: am I engaging in these behaviors? Can you think of any other indications?

Hope at work

> People of hope are always people who so embrace the promise that they will not settle for present circumstance. ~ Walter Brueggemann

Hope means anything but passivity. Hope does not mean waiting passively for a desired outcome. True hope moves us to action.

"We do not hope for what we have," said Thomas Merton. "Therefore, to live in hope is to live in poverty, having nothing." This sounds about right for a guy who lived in a monastery and took a vow of poverty. It even sounds poetic. But watch out for Merton—no, wait—watch out for hope, because it's full of surprises. In *No Man Is An Island*, Merton went on to reflect about hope-filled poverty:

> *Hope is appropriate to detachment. It brings our souls into the state of the most perfect detachment. In doing so, it restores all values by setting them in their right order. Hope empties our hands in order that we may work with them. It shows us that we have something to work for, and teaches us how to work for it.*

I like this passage because Merton helps me see things in a new light: my empty hands mean I am free to work with them. When my hands are full—full of possessions, anxieties, and the stuff of life—I am not free to work, to build, to create, to share, to love. How foolish to define *the good life* as a life filled with things! We rent storage space or build bigger barns to hold these possessions. We insure our possessions against loss and install "security systems" to deter thieves. But there is no such thing as a system of security. Hope in something beyond myself takes me beyond myself. Hope leads to work not because work is a means to acquiring things but because work is the practical expression of hope.

John Polkinghorne is a unique example of hope at work. A theoretical physicist, he is also a theologian, a writer, and an Anglican priest. He's written five books on physics—and *26 books* on the relationship between science and faith. "Hope is much more than a mood," he writes. "It is a commitment to action . . . What we hope for should be what we are prepared to work for, as far as that power lies within us." Polkinghorne is not urging us to work in order to possess, he is suggesting the possibility that hope is the only motivation that fuels us in our life's purpose.

True hope is effective hope. It is the virtue that moves us to action as we become aware of the tremendous trust God puts in us by making promises to us. His promises remind us that he will do what only he can do, but these same promises birth in us the kind of hope that strengthens us to act.

Farmers understand this kind of hope. In the cold of winter they prepare for spring: repairing equipment, borrowing money for Spring planting—all the while fully aware that no amount of responsible preparation can guarantee success. But they know the promise of spring rains, summer sun, and the joy of fall's harvest. They've taken to heart God's promise, spoken over all creation:

As long as the earth endures,
  seedtime and harvest, cold and heat,
summer and winter, day and night,
  shall not cease." (Genesis 8:22)

But this romantic view of farming is not enough. Rains can be delayed—or come in a violent flood. The sun can shine without mercy and scorch the earth. Even the most bountiful harvest must be gathered in a timely way, or the fruit with rot on the vine. Anyone who works the land understands the dance between hope and labor. True hope calls forth our best efforts. Merton again:

"If I hope in God, I must also make a confident use of the natural aids which, with grace, enable me to come to him. If he is good, and if my intelligence is his gift, then I will show my trust in his goodness by making use of my intelligence . . . Some who think they trust in God actually sin against hope because they do not use the will and the judgment he has given them. Of what use is it for me to hope in grace if I dare not make the act of will that corresponds with grace? How do I profit by abandoning myself passively to his will if I lack the strength of will to obey his commands? Therefore, if I trust in God's grace I must also show confidence in the natural powers he has given me, not because they are my powers but because they are his gift."

Only those who hope can work as free men and women. All others are slaves to futility; they work because the whip of need drives them forward. People of hope and not driven forward, they are pursuing the promise of the future.

I'm left asking myself some questions: has my passivity caused me to sin against hope? In what practical ways should I respond to God's promises? Could my strong hope be the difference between fatigue and the strength to finish the work given me by God?

Strange Day on a City Bus

No matter how dark the moment, love and hope are always possible. ~ George Chakiris

I was waiting for a bus and a guy sat down next to me. You know that uncomfortable distance between two strangers forced to share a bench? He began to chat but I wasn't looking at me.

> *Hope is for fools. Hope is the language of the disorganized, the misfits, and those losers who feel the need to redefine winning into something that isn't winning at all. Everyone knows it. Life is really all about winning. It's a hashtag. It's rap chorus: "All I do is win, win, win." Winning means great ideas, insightful strategies, relentless effort, and flawless execution. But hope is not a strategy.*
>
> *On the other hand the Internet loves hope, perhaps because memes cost nothing to make, nothing to share, and no one remembers a meme ten minutes after we've scrolled past it. On social media hope comes to us in soft-focus photography, gauzy filters over pastel colors, and fonts that flow from an old-fashioned quill pen.*

I decided to name this guy "Gary" because I figured there was no way he was ever going to introduce himself to me.

> *It's not very practical. Hope is like autumn leaves in their beautiful colors. No, that's not right: it's like autumn leaves after they fall and we hear them sweep across the concrete sidewalk or gather in heap at the gutter. Hope allows children to play*

53

in the leaves and be happy for a few moments. But only a few moments. The frost is coming to stay. The leaves don't even make good kindling in a fireplace. And memories won't keep anyone warm. But the practical, hard work of splitting wood does, though. And you can stack it on the porch and use it all winter.

Honestly, what good is hope? It's good for greeting cards. It's good for white lies whispered to people in hospice. It's good for sharing comfort without anyone taking the responsibility to make anything happen.

Gary went quiet for a moment. There, at the bus stop, I just turned my head and looked at him. But I didn't say anything. He looked back at me, and then continued:

Most people can't define it.

Ask the next ten people you meet, "What does 'hope' mean to you?" They will stare a little blankly and wonder if you're serious. If they choose to play your game they will start out with a definition but quickly get bogged down into talking about darkness and despair. I know, because I've asked lots of people. Their definitions jumble out in a tumble of flowery words but it's amazing how many people move right into a stories bout the death of a loved one or opportunities missed or about how someone acted on a foolish whim and came away with a handful of smoke. People are afraid to talk about hope—I mean real hope, the kind that costs them something.

How many people understand hope? They'll say you can't do without it but they'll never be able to explain what, exactly, you can do with it.

Hope is the refuge of the powerless; it's a circle of metal folding chairs arranged on a tile floor in a church basement. We drink bad coffee and tell our stories and think we are actually getting something done. Hope works out for the guy on the other side of the circle. He says his sister's son was staring at a stage four diagnosis but dared to hope and now everything's all better. You want to lean into the group and ask, "Wait a minute: how—exactly—did this invisible nephew translate hope into some kind of action or choice?" The rest of the people in the circle change their posture and the group leader reminds you that inside the circle we speak only uplifting comments. You don't want to hear about other people, though: you're looking for hope for you. Why else would you ride across town to sit in a church basement and listen to people who have it as bad as you?

The bus pulled up and Gary followed me up the steps. I don't think he ever stopped talking. I don't even think he knew which bus he boarded.

It's only on the ride back home that you realize you've missed the point: where else would hope hang out? It's certainly not at Nordstroms among all the quality products displayed for the winners who can afford them. Then you remember that one of the guys in the circle was wearing $200 shoes and wearing a Rolex, but he hadn't shaved in three days and couldn't lift his eyes off the square vinyl tiles. He had to come to a place where his money was no good, and that's a price he was willing to pay. A price that came with no guarantees or return privileges. The most he could do was stuff a twenty

55

in the coffee jar and hope that next week they'd
brew something other than Folgers.
That's when I noticed his $200 shoes and Rolex. He
hadn't shaved in three days. I ventured a question:
"Why do you do it?" But he didn't hear me, or if he did
he thought I was the voice inside his head.

Then you begin to ask yourself why some
people came to the meeting every week and (who
knows?) maybe even went to two other meetings in
the days between. Because this is where hope lives.
It lives in the hum of florescent lighting and the
washed-out faces of people who no longer care
how they look or what you think of them. They
didn't join the circle to impress you; they came
because there was a chance—a chance—to find
hope.
Here's the thing about hope. It's what everyone
is willing to offer others but what we secretly hope
we will never need. If you're down to hope, you're
down to nothing. Then you realize that hope is a
part of that nothing. You're whispering to yourself
not to go too far and drink the caffeinated Kool-Aid
because you know darned well that you're just
fooling yourself and saying what you think they
want you to say.
Then he pulled the buzzer-cord that tells the driver to
stop at the corner—the corner where an old stone
church stood with a discrete little sign that pointed to a
side entrance. The kind of entrance where people
without hope can slip in, undetected. He stepped off
the bus. I watched him disappear around the side of the
building. I prayed a quick prayer for the guy drunk on
cynicism, but who was at least willing to walk the
twelve steps.

56

Hope for Change

"Hope is a movement of the soul." ~ Aquinas

Life in Christ is constant transformation. Because we follow an infinite Lord, our possibilities are infinite as well. Becoming a follower of Jesus should bring three transformations: we are born from above, we can acquire his character, and we can imitate his works. Most believers North America have some grasp on the first, a hope of the second, and almost no concept of the third.

The gospel stories reveal a ragtag group of Jesus-followers beset with infighting and petty pride. Yet as Jesus prepared to leave he charged these struggling men with the impossible.

"I tell you the truth, anyone who has faith in me will do what I have been doing. He will do even greater things than these, because I am going to the Father. And I will do whatever you ask in my name, so that the Son may bring glory to the Father. You may ask me for anything in my name, and I will do it." (John 14:12-14)

The first disciples demonstrated they were up to the task—not because they had their act together, but because the life of Jesus had been planted in them as an imperishable seed. The seed would grow within them:

1). The first disciples found themselves transformed by the new birth. They really were a new creation.

Heaven's DNA had altered their very being. Formerly timid, self-absorbed, working-class men threatened the Roman Empire just as their Master had done. If we have the family DNA, where is the family resemblance? Modern Christians are troubled by their past, troubled by their sin, and troubled by their future. They've experienced little or no change. But if the power of God can assure our eternal destiny, shouldn't it be able to impact our thoughts and actions here and now? That was the record of the early church.

2). *The first disciples found themselves transformed in character.* They demonstrated the character of Christ to a degree not possible by their own good intentions or human effort. In our day, we are tempted to think we should "act better" because we are Christians. It's a trap: we will only "act better" as long as our will power holds up—just ask anyone who has ever started a diet! Eventually our mere willpower will fail us even as it failed the disciples the night Jesus was arrested. True character change flows from the new birth the way spring water flows from the source. The transformation of new birth finds its way into our character by the hunger and thirst for the stuff of heaven. A newborn child without hunger or thirst is desperately ill: why should it be any different in our life with Christ?

3). *The first disciples found themselves transformed by power for ministry.* The first followers of Jesus were startlingly like Jesus in thought, word, and *deed.* Ordinary people declared the message of the Kingdom of God (as Jesus had done) and *demonstrated* the coming of that Kingdom with powerful actions (just as Jesus had done). By the Holy Spirit the first believers discovered a transformation from the impossibilities of the flesh to the possibilities of heaven. What does it mean to do the works of Jesus? How we answer the question reveals our understanding of what it means to live "in Christ." In his day, Jesus had a high view of his followers. He believed in them more than they believed in themselves. It's *still* his day if we will let him have his way.

The first disciples were up to the task. In the intervening centuries the people of God have sometimes lived up to the charge left by our Lord, and sometimes have exchanged heavenly tasks into something attainable by human effort. Every generation must wrestle with the challenge Jesus left us. The first disciples were up to the task. The question is whether we are up to the task as well.

God's Economy Runs on Hope

"Your hopes will always outstrip your resources." ~ Adam Russell

I took a couple of economics classes when I was in school but only later did I learn that the study of Economics is called *The Dismal Science*. One of the earliest economists, Robert Malthus, was certainly dismal. He warned that because the increase in human population would outpace human production of food, mankind was doomed to unending poverty and hardship. It was 1798, and he predicted death and starvation in the coming century.

I suspect the well-meaning textbooks missed the point. I've come to see that whether we spend dollars or euros, the truth is that every economy in the world actually runs on scarcity and fear. From the kitchen table at home to each table in the board rooms of every corporation, we hear the spoon scraping the jar, and fear rises up: that we will not have enough peanut butter or investment capital; that we will not have enough income after taxes or will we miss the limited opportunity the marketplace affords. It's one reason why—no matter what our income or our standard of living—we live with an unsettling fear that whatever we have, it's not enough.

Scarcity pulls the lever of fear, and fear moves us to action. "Put your money in land," advised Will Rogers, "because they aren't making any more of it." This was good advice—right up until real estate values plummeted in the last decade. Some years ago, when Apple Corporation began buying back its own shares of stock, investment counselors told their clients to buy Apple shares as well, because the number of available shares was declining. Apple stock was becoming scarce! (Actually, there are more than three *billion* shares of Apple stock—how many shares are enough?) If the weather forecast calls for snow the local grocery store can expect a run on bread and milk. (Personally, I'd stock up on donuts and coffee, but that's just me.) We believe in this thinking so strongly we've begun to describe these ideas as forces of nature; the "laws of supply and demand" have the same power as gravity or the tides of the sea.

I wonder if we can imagine a world where the most valuable things are in infinite supply, where scarcity and fear do not drive our actions. Can we catch a glimpse of an existence where some things last forever, a kind of life where the most valuable things we have multiply as we give them away? What if there are inexhaustible resources of those things we need most? So it is with faith, hope, and love.

Hope at Prayer

One day Jesus was praying in a certain place. When he finished, one of his disciples said to him, "Lord, teach us to pray, just as John taught his disciples."(Luke 11:1)

Have you ever asked someone a question and then stopped listening too soon? The disciples asked Jesus for a lesson on prayer, but many of us quit listening after the first few verses. His answer stretches all the way to verse 13.

After Jesus provided a sample prayer he continued with seven simple words that can forever change our idea of prayer: "*Suppose one of you has a friend . . .*" (Luke 11: 5) Jesus moved the conversation from the *content* of prayer to the *relationship* between God and man. He calls the relationship *friendship*.

Some friendships stand on stick-legs: they can't hold much weight. Every conversation has to be measured carefully to avoid damaging the relationship. Jesus, on the other hand, presents the example of a friendship so strong that both men can say exactly what they think without any worry of ruining their bond.

The story is of two men who knew each other so well they could be completely honest. One guy receives an unexpected visitor late at night and needs to provide hospitality. He goes to his friend's house—even though it's too late at night to drop by—and asks for extra food.

His friend says, "Are you nuts? It's way too late, come back tomorrow."

Yet the relationship is so strong that the first guy can say, "I'm not leaving until I get what I need."

Bible scholars will tell you that Jesus paints this picture to illustrate the importance of persistence in prayer, and of course that's true. But there's something more: Jesus invites us to imagine prayer as an extension of honest, real friendship. If we approach prayer academically we will rush past Jesus' simple introduction, *"Suppose you have a friend."* He asks us to draw on our experience and imagine the best friendship we have, then apply that kind of security and strength to the way we talk to God.

The point of his illustration is that friendship itself is the reason we can persist. The reason we can be so bold to knock on the door at midnight is that we know our rude behavior will not sever the relationship. We can continue to ask, seek, and knock because we know the heart of the one we are bothering. He's our friend. The kind of friend for whom the rules don't count. I'd like to suggest at least five thoughts that may change your prayers:

We don't have to wait for the proper time to come and ask. If the situation calls for it, bang on the door in the middle of the night. That's what real friends are for.

The friendship door swings both ways: the second friend is comfortable in the relationship, too. So comfortable, in fact, that the first answer might be, "Don't bother me!" Does our picture of God allow for the possibility that I could press through the first answer? Would *you* ever ask God to change his mind?

When my friend does answer, **he will give me "as much as I need**." Friends don't keep score: what's yours is mine, and vice versa. The basis for his generosity is the relationship, not the rules of etiquette.

I can have the boldness to keep on asking when I'm asking on behalf of someone else. Remember how the story starts? There's a third party in the picture. They are the ones who will eat the bread; they are the ones in need. Jesus is suggesting that when we pray out of our need to bless others, God is more than generous, but how many times have I limited my prayers to my needs?

Finally, **Jesus is unafraid to mix metaphors**. Just as the power of this imaginary scene is beginning to sink in, Jesus begins to talk about fathers, children, and the Holy Spirit (vs 11- 13). Can we turn our imagination in still more directions? Perhaps, but that's another chapter in the story of hope.

Reflection #3

Think of someone you do not like. Not a public figure, a personal one; that man or woman who drives you crazy. You wonder: *does he stay awake at night thinking of ways to annoy me?* (The good news is that he probably does not. The bad news is that he annoys you quite naturally, without working at it!)

Now, take a deep breath, and ask the Father for the grace to lay aside your frustration and judgment concerning this person. Ask the Holy Spirit to open your imagination, like this: try to imagine what are *God's hopes* for this person. When the Creator fashioned this man, this woman, what was in God's heart toward him or her? The Maker had something in mind for this person, some potential, some calling, some great destiny. By divine grace, try to lay hold of God's hopes for this annoying person.

Finally, as you catch a glimpse of God's hope for this person, turn the revelation into prayer. Pray God's great hopes for this person, that he or she will receive and become all they were created to be. Instead of asking God to "fix" this person, why not ask God to fulfill the hope of His destiny for them.

For advanced students: move beyond the person who merely annoys you. Can you pray like this for your enemies?

The Scent of Hope

But thanks be to God, who always leads us as captives in Christ's triumphal procession and uses us to spread the aroma of the knowledge of him everywhere. For we are to God the pleasing aroma of Christ among those who are being saved and those who are perishing. To the one we are an aroma that brings death; to the other, an aroma that brings life. And who is equal to such a task? ~ 2 Corinthians 2:14-16

Perhaps it's the smell of donuts and tea, all yeasty and sweet. Or roses: nuanced and subtle, filling the room. Or the smell of baking bread where there should be the stench of burning flesh. Of course, the Apostle Paul was only using a metaphor, right? The intellectual colossus of Christianity would have never intended we could actually smell the presence of Jesus, would he?

I was away on a business trip last week. My 8 year-old daughter used my Cheerios Tee as a nightshirt, but not before smelling all the T-shirts in the closet because they reminded her of Daddy. We could never remember Jesus like that. Never? Widows tell of opening a dresser drawer and catching the fragrance of their husband long departed. Our brain recalls the decades past by the faintest whiff of a meal we ate as children. We smell the beach before we see the ocean.

Check the commentaries and you'll find the musty smell of books and study. The commentators will remind you of Roman processions and temples filled with incense. The learned professors will explain these words were the stuff of Paul's creative metaphor.

But there is another way: you can check the history of the people of God, common folk who have experienced uncommon things:

John the Apostle had a disciple named Polycarp. In 155 A.D. he was arrested and threatened with fire because he loved John's Master, Jesus. "You threaten fire which burns for an hour and is soon quenched." he said. "Why do you wait? Come, do what you will!" When the authorities tied him to a stake and set him ablaze, his skin turned golden brown and witnesses smelled the smell of baking bread. Since the witnesses were not theologians they reported their experience and not a metaphor: the aroma of the bread of life.But who can trust witnesses dead for 18 centuries? Something like that could never happen today.

That's what I thought until a gnarly old musician, a 60's throwback who sang worship songs to Jesus came to our little town. Barely 40 people gathered to hear him sing and minister. Yet when he prayed one-on-one for those who stayed until the end, the room swelled with rose-scent, a bouquet of God's presence right before my very nose. It happened again the next day as I drove him to the airport. Our car filled with perfume as if an alabaster jar had been broken before me.

Still, it's hard to believe, I grant you. And who could possibly expect it to happen again? Until one Sunday morning when two rows of worshipers in our church encountered the smell of donuts and tea while they sang and raised their hands, each one sure they were the only ones until one looked at another and said, "This is weird, but do you smell tea?"

Of course, the commentators are right: Paul's words are allusions to the practices of the day. He was merely drawing on the common understanding of his times. But what if Paul also wrote his experiences down? What if there is also a spiritual reality long lost, and the Holy Spirit still brings the scent of hope?

The Leaven of Hope

To live without Hope is to cease to live. ~
Fyodor Dostoyevsky

My first workplace nickname was *Doughboy.* Not because I was chubby: it was because of my two-year relationship with dough balls. I worked at a hole-in-the-wall pizza joint near the racetrack in Arlington Heights, Illinois. (Think of *The Princess Bride,* where Robin Wright uses the name *Farmboy* for Cary Elwes, but then take away the farm and Robin Wright and replace it all with cold florescent lights above an ugly kitchen: "Doughboy, fetch me that pail.")

Each day I arrived an hour before the others and mixed a fresh batch of dough. Two huge 25-pound sacks of flour. Quarts and quarts of water. Sugar. Salt. And a *tiny* package of yeast. The commercial mixer groaned and whirred until the collection of powders and water gave off a sticky sweet smell. It turned and turned until the ingredients became dough—lots of it. I reached into the mixer and pulled out handfuls of pizza dough and measured them into six- ounce dough balls, four wide and six long on a stainless steel tray. The dough balls, made by the Doughboy, became the foundation for the perfect food—pizza. Nor was my work finished. I had to re-shape the dough balls twice each night because the yeast caused them to grow more than twice the size of the original six-ounce lump.

Later, as I began to read the New Testament, I discovered in Mathew 13 that Jesus already knew my occupation and nickname:

> He told them still another parable: "The kingdom of heaven is like yeast that a woman took and mixed into about fifty pounds of flour until it worked all through the dough." (Except the woman didn't have the advantage of a commercial mixer!)

I had seen it firsthand: the yeast was the last ingredient, the tiniest amount, but it made the dough come alive. This is the way of the kingdom. The smallest things have great effects. Leaven, a microscopic lifeless dust, comes to life in the right moment and the right environment. Resurrection performed nightly at the pizza joint.

In a rare moment of clarity I grasped his point the first time I heard it. The hidden work of God is inexorable. Whether it's a new birth or a new idea, he finds a way in us and through us. The secret ingredient is life from another realm. It finds a way.

Jesus the storyteller reveals the workings of the kingdom. Yeast, mustard seed, wheat and weeds, even beams of light: each starts with God's action in us, planting and placing, shining upon us until each ingredient shines forth from us. I learned something of his method. It is hidden, and it is hidden in us. We are the environment of God's activity. He breaks off a piece of himself and hides it deep within us. We discover it, nurture it, and eventually we share it with our world. He submerses himself in us so deeply we can easily miss his presence, even though it's the animating force behind our rising.

Night after night in a no-account pizza joint, the work of God was played out before me. I learned to trust the yeast even if I couldn't see it working. In truth, I couldn't stop it if I wanted to.

And it's not only true about me. It's true for each of his children. The superstars are not the only ones who will rise. Through each of us God is at work in a thousand ways, and we are delivered all over town. I've learned to trust the leaven in others as well—in the right time each kingdom child will shine like the sun. We are the aroma of Christ to a perishing world. Resurrection nightly, not just at the end of days.

And while we wait, we are in on the secret. The leaven is here, in us, rising.

Changing Faith, Constant Hope

"Hope is not something that happens to us. It's not a warm possible feeling about the future; it is a virtue we must train ourselves to engage with." ~ Dan Wilt

Almost no one uses a grandfather clock these days, but that doesn't mean the pendulum isn't busy swinging back and forth. There is a back-and-forth sway of popular ideas in society—and in the society of God's people, known as the church.

My first twenty years with God I was surrounded by the need for faith, expressed in plain Evangelical language. Saint Billy Graham provided a fine bumper-sticker example: *"God said it. I believe it. That settles it."* Bible-teacher Derek Prince intoned, *"All progress in the Christian walk is by faith."* Both sayings are true, but the pull of groupthink created an environment where faith morphed into a powerful orthodoxy of agreement. We all boldly proclaimed our faith—even when we didn't quite believe it.

My second twenty years with God saw the invisible pendulum swing the opposite way. Honest doubt became the password of authenticity. Certainty became the sign of arrogance. The cyber community reminded us the difference between someone's interpretation of the Bible and "Bible truth." They demonstrated how doubt could lead to spiritual growth. *"I believe—help me in my unbelief'* became a popular topic among emerging church leaders. But the pull of groupthink worked here as well. Although doubt is often a useful path for discovery, it became the approved approach to faith: don't trust anyone who is firm in his or her beliefs. The only "honest" position is doubt.

I have great hope for the next few years. Perhaps we can live for a while in the center, a place of humble certainty.

We can find the place of humble certainty if we embrace the need and the blessings of faith while holding our doubts and fears honestly without making them into a virtue.

Consider these very challenging words from John's gospel, the very last message of the book: "these things are written that you may believe that Jesus is the Messiah, the Son of God, and that by believing you may have life in his name. There's a deep connection between believing and receiving a divine quality of life. The final phrase, "that by believing you may have life" is about something more than going to Heaven; it's about the quality of life available to us here and now.

Make no mistake: it takes faith to experience this kind of life. Without faith, the flow of divine life is choked to a trickle. Not a faith in propositions, or political positions, or even correct doctrines, but a trusting relationship with a living person, Jesus. In my first twenty years I was told faith meant following a line of behaviors or practices that "proved" my commitment. In my second twenty years I've been told that doubt is the only honest kind of faith. In my first twenty years the Apostle Peter was my example; in the second twenty it was Doubting Thomas. But neither Peter nor

Thomas give life. Life comes from only one man, Jesus, the Messiah, the Son of God.

If the pendulum is entering the radical middle, perhaps we can re-define faith as trust—the kind of trust that flourishes between two people when they share life together. That's the faith/trust I want with Jesus. To the degree I experience the divine life of peace, that's the measure of my faith. How about you? Can you live in the center?

Against Hope, In Hope

Against all hope, Abraham in hope believed and so became the father of many nations, just as it had been said to him, "So shall your offspring be." Without weakening in his faith, he faced the fact that his body was as good as dead—since he was about a hundred years old—and that Sarah's womb was also dead. Yet he did not waver through unbelief regarding the promise of God, but was strengthened in his faith and gave glory to God, being fully persuaded that God had power to do what he had promised. ~ Romans 4:18-21

"He faced the fact that his body was a good as dead." I love this. It tells me that faith does not require that I ignore the facts. I can stare frankly at what is before me. At the same time there are things bigger than the facts. This passage teaches me I can acknowledge my doubts without celebrating them.

"Being fully persuaded that God had power to do what he had promised." Verses 20 and 21 tell me that Abraham's faith rested in God's promises, not a limited understanding of the situation. In fact, Abraham was persuaded that God *could* and *would* act. I suspect the reason faith is difficult for some people is that they've been told faith is believing a set of theological "facts" instead of trusting a person—a person fully capable and willing to acting on their behalf.

In another New Testament book Peter said that we become partakers in the divine nature through God's promises. His promises give us hope. That hope whispers to us, "go ahead—dare to to trust him, and to trust his promise!" I want nothing to do with a definition of faith that requires agreement with propositions and everything to do with a faith that requires me to hope and trust in the Father's promise.

Perhaps you could consider this during the week: faith is not agreeing with a set of propositions, it's knowing a Person, hearing His promises, and trusting Him to fulfill them. Surely that's better than celebrating my doubt, isn't it?

When Solomon, who confined himself to matters under the sun, intoned, "*with much wisdom comes much sorrow; the more knowledge, the more grief,*" he forever linked the idea that serious people were sad because disillusionment is the only choice of the enlightened. Camus, Satre, Voltaire (anyone from France, really) and most great thinkers have fallen in line with the fallen king of Israel. The wisdom of the wise is to expect disappointment, anticipate disaster, and gainsay anyone who prefers sunrise to sunset.

The worldly-wise require a dreary realism for club membership. The doorman greets the cynic, but keeps the hopeful behind the velvet rope. "Happy people are hopeless," they say. "Hopelessly idealistic and hopelessly romantic." In fact, the exact opposite is true: happy people are the hope-filled, the joy-saturated, the ones so full of the Spirit he oozes out of them. The surprising testimony of the scripture, and the Lord of the scripture, is that history has a destination of unspeakable joy.

Even when we look cold-hard at the suffering of a desperate world, we can see the text of God superimposed on the landscape, written with a feather-touch: *"the sufferings of this present time are not worthy to be compared with the glory that is to be revealed to us."* Let's meditate on the fruit of the Spirit, those nine attributes I can never seem to remember in order: love, joy, peace, patience, kindness, goodness, faithfulness, gentleness and self-control. Discover again with me that "serious" is not a fruit of the Spirit.

The shipwrecked and beaten apostle reminds us, *"against such things there is no law."* They cannot be legislated into existence, nor regulated out. They can only be lived into. They can only be discovered as the natural outgrowth of a life lived in concert with the Great Creator, the Feast-throwing Father, the one who invites us, "enter into the joy of your Master."

Cheap Hope

"Hope remains if friends stay true."

~ J.R.R. Tolkien.

For each heavenly virtue and gift there is a deception and counterfeit. Just as Dieterich Bonhoeffer spoke of *cheap grace*, there is such a thing as cheap hope. Human optimism is cheap hope. When hope departs from the truth and fails to factor in divine mercy, it becomes cheap hope. Cheap hope is easy to give away because it has no real value.

Cheap hope is what we offer to others when we do not know what else to say. There, at the hospital bedside, where tubes and wires and monitors all testify to the seriousness of the situation, we feel the fear of death rising up in us. We turn to cheap hope to comfort ourselves, not the person in the bed. "Don't worry," we say. "God has everything under control." Where do we learn such sentences? And do we really believe them ourselves? Cheap hope makes us feel better even while it diminishes the suffering of others. Cheap hope is when we speak words of encouragement to others while we ourselves avoid the hard work facing the facts. Cheap hope allows us to leave the hospital feeling good about ourselves because we have paid a visit to the sick. We have earned points with God and comforted ourselves.

Positive thinking is not hope. Hope does the hard work of facing the facts. Hope knows the odds. Cheap hope oversells the good news and subtly ignores the bad news—but hope cannot be hope if we refuse to see things the way they really are. Our great examples are Abraham and Sarah. God promised them a son, but Abraham and Sarah were too old for such foolishness. Sarah laughed at the idea, and Abraham was well aware of his old age. Cheap hope invites us to jump ahead to the happy ending, but before we leap to the promised fulfilled, let's consider how ridiculous the situation was. The Apostle Paul taught us how to do the hard work: "In hope against hope he believed," he says of Abraham. "Without becoming weak in faith he contemplated his own body, now as good as dead since he was about a hundred years old, and the deadness of Sarah's womb; yet, with respect to the promise of God, he did not waver in unbelief but grew strong in faith." Paul is teaching us that faith and hope do not ignore the facts; faith and hope face them.

In his thoughtful book, *The Anatomy of Hope*, Dr. Jermone Groopman shares his journey from cheap hope to strong, solid, true hope. Groopman is an oncologist—a specialty that stares into the face of cancer every day. Early in his career Groopman treated a mother, Frances, for Stage D colon cancer. Frances was always accompanied by her college-age daughter, Sharon, who was intelligent and brave. Young Dr. Groopman made the choice to deliver cheap hope: he talked with mother and daughter about all the advances in oncology and all the treatment options available. He never shared the odds. In his medical training he had been coached to believe "sustained ignorance is bliss" for a terminal patient. Frances died. Her daughter, Sharon, confronted Groopman. She did not complain about the treatment, but rather about his choice to obscure the hard news: "I guess [you] didn't think people like us were smart enough, or strong enough, to handle the truth." Groopman realized his error: "[I doubted] whether Frances and Sharon were capable of hope." He realized he "doubted not only the resilience of my patient but also my own capacity for hope . . . I never gave Frances or Sharon the opportunity to choose what to hope for."

Groopman's book tells the story of his journey as both a doctor and as one who discovered the difference between cheap hope and true hope. Cheap hope is a deception, but that does mean there is no such thing as true hope. Courageous hope "helps us overcome the hurdles we otherwise could not scale, and it moves us forward to a place where healing can occur . . . [It] is the ballast that keeps us steady, that recognizes where along the path are the dangers and pitfalls that can throw us off; hope tempers fear so we can recognize that dangers and then bypass or endure them."

Cheap hope is the fearful man whistling past the graveyard. He's not afraid of ghosts; he's afraid the cemetery has a plot reserved for him. True hope looks at the facts, counts the cost, and refuses the quick and easy answer. True hope requires a clear head and a courageous heart.

Hope & Hell

"Let those who dread be allowed to hope."

~ Lucan

Dante Alighieri lived and died more than seven centuries ago. To this day the Italian poet is considered the bright star of the Medieval period and a precursor of the Renaissance. Yet he was also a failed politician who found himself exiled from Florence, a brilliant man who carried the pain of failure and rejection with him as he left. His pain—and his bitterness—found it's way into his *Divine Comedy*, a massive poem that takes us on a tour of Hell, Purgatory, and Heaven. Many of our modern religious ideas about Hell come from Dante's *Inferno*, the first part of the *Divine Comedy*. It's famous: and this poem is a part of your image of Hell, whether you've read it or not. It's filled with punishment and suffering—people who get what they deserve! Nearly everyone Dante hates ends up in Hell, all of them receiving custom-made tortures and retribution. The *Inferno* is the ultimate score-settling fantasy.

Near the beginning of the poem he depicts dreadful sign posted above the gates of Hell: *ABANDON HOPE ALL YE WHO ENTER HERE*. It's chilling to read, even now. But the sign is not actually true; it's an attempt at intimidation. The power of Hell is found in the absence of hope. The way into Hell is the abandonment of hope. Hell is not hopeless; hopelessness is Hell. Hell is the loss of hope.

Thomas Merton, a man whose spirituality took a decidedly different path, said, "The damned have confirmed themselves in the belief that they cannot hope in God." I'm with Merton over Dante. The practical side of Merton's observation is that, for many people, Hell is closer than we think. Hell isn't the punishment of some angry god; Hell is where we find ourselves when we lose Heaven's gift, hope.

OK, yes, this is heavy reading, right? Hell, damnation, torture, and suffering! Right about now you're thinking, "he's a real buzz-kill at parties." Fine. Don't invite me to your party, but do keep this in front of you: hope is ours to keep, to tend, to care for. We are the stewards of hope, both for ourselves and for those around us. What if Hell isn't a destination, but an awful affliction experienced day-by-day? What if those who are suffering in this life engage in binge-eating, or credit card-spending, or drunkenness, or any other out-of-balance behavior as a substitute for hope?

The scripture describes God as "the God of hope," and if you count yourself among the people of God, then you are a caretaker, a steward of his hope. Not only should we carefully steward hope for ourselves, we should also share hope as an invitation to others. We bear the message of hope, and extend it to others, a rescue for others. The Apostle Paul, himself a guardian of hope, described his ministry like this:

> But we have this treasure in earthen vessels, so that the surpassing greatness of the power will be of God and not from ourselves; we are afflicted in every way, but not crushed; perplexed, but not despairing; persecuted, but not forsaken; struck down, but not destroyed; always carrying about in the body the dying of Jesus, so that the life of Jesus

also may be manifested in our body. For we who alive are constantly being delivered over to death for Jesus' sake, so that the life of Jesus also may be manifested in our mortal flesh. So death works in us, but life in you. (2 Corinthians 4:7-12)

I like to think of Paul as the vessel and hope as the precious oil within the vessel. He saw his weakness and hardships—even his injuries—as the means by which hope reached other people.

Today, Dante and his fundamentalist forebears will continue to consign their enemies to Hell. Jesus, on the other hand, descended into Hell and led a host of people back into the light.   We should, too. True children of God, broken, cracked, and bruised though we are, imperfect vessels that we most certainly are, will bear the oil of hope to a world that finds itself already in Hell.

A Hope-filled Way to Read the Scriptures

"Love is not without hope, hope is not without love, and neither hope nor love are without faith." ~ Augustine of Hippo

I have a friend who says that the only thing he ever gets from reading the Bible is sleepy. I have another friend who reads the Bible like a lawyer. She sees the Bible as a book of rules and God as the Ultimate Judge. I have one more friend, a songwriter, who reads the Bible like a poet, and it will come as no surprise that he finds the Bible filled with beauty and mystery. Guess which friend I enjoy hanging out with?

Since Hope deals with things unseen, it requires a little imagination to read the Bible in a Hope-filled way. I'd like to suggest four ways to engage the inspired text with our imagination.

Imagine the setting. Jesus worked and taught in a real world. He walked real hillsides and felt the heat of the day on his body. The Son of God sweat. He thirsted. One way to hear the word of God anew is to put yourself into the setting. You needn't be a Biblical archeologist to do so: the important thing is to take the words off the page and wrap yourself in the setting. The fun-loving guys of Monty Python imagined what it must've been like for those who found themselves on the outermost edge of the crowd listening to the Sermon on the Mount, straining to hear a far-away voice. ("Blessed are the cheesemakers?!? What does that mean?") Their imagination inspired laughter. What could yours inspire?

Join the party: You don't need an engraved invitation. Come in, sit down, and put yourself in the setting. It does no disrespect to the Biblical narrative to add one more person to the scene. You could be the thirteenth disciple. Or the woman with five husbands. Or the rich young ruler. Dallas Willard observed that one of the first steps in hearing God in the scripture is the ability to recognize that the people of the Bible were real people, no different from you or me. Even the narrative sections of the scripture are addressed to us personally. The trick is to re-create the setting, then accept the invitation to the party.

Stay yourself, be real: Jesus isn't speaking to other people, he's speaking to you. Each person who heard the actual words of Jesus was a real person with a real life. This one was fisherman, who thought and responded like a working man. That one was a wife and a mother, who thought and acted in ways very different from a fisherman. If the words of Jesus are truly the word of God, they should speak to us where we are: man, woman, rich, poor, depressed, confident, gay, straight, black, white, Asian, Latin, rested, fatigued, desperate or self-sufficient. Some people engage in conversation while others ponder words in their heart. Howwould *you* have reacted if you were actually there, listening to him speak? A stained-glass answer will not do, only a real answer prepares our heart for the word.

Respond to the word: Perhaps you've never noticed it, but *everyone in the Biblical narrative responded to the* *word of God.* The rich young ruler went away unhappy; the woman at the well returned to town and told everyone how her life had changed. The implicit message of the Biblical narratives is simply you cannot walk away from the word of God unchanged. Yet modern readers of the Bible close the book and walk away unaffected. It's the difference between an intellectual exercise and experiencing his words. It's the difference between reading and living the word.

Hope comes from an imaginative engagement with the word of God. If we place ourselves in the text, we begin to imagine ourselves as real people, engaging with a real Lord. After all, we're real, aren't we? He's risen and real, isn't he? An *imaginative encounter* with the text produces hope because we *imagine ourselves* differently as a result of meeting Jesus. It's just another way of saying, "the inbreaking of your word brings light."

Hope on Netflix

That's what we storytellers do. We restore order
with imagination and instill hope again, and
again, and again. ~ Walt Disney

Call me Nancy. Whenever I find myself growing grim
about the mouth, whenever it is a damp, drizzly,
November in my soul, then I account it high time to
watch *Under the Tuscan Sun*. It may cost me my man-
card, but I turn to Diane Lane and the unlikely family
gathered around her to embrace again feelings of faith,
hope, and love. Come with me.

Audrey Wells' adaptation of the Frances Mayes memoir
probably didn't target the melancholy middle-aged
male demographic, but it hits he spot for me. It tells the
story of an American writer who buys a broken-down
Tuscan villa, even as she is recovering from a divorce,
and engages on a restoration project. Both the writer
and the villa are restored in due course.

Along the way we meet a real estate broker with the
heart of St. Francis of Assisi, a gaggle of Polish
construction workers in varied states of emotional
distress, and a jilted pregnant lesbian best-friend—all of
whom comprise the family gathered around Frances—
herself a bit of a work in progress. It doesn't hurt at all
that Frances is played by Diane Lane, the thinking-
man's Hollywood beauty (I say this because I found a
thinking man and asked his opinion).

Spiritual references are added to the film like
seasoning: nuns who toddle through various scenes like

a waddle of penguins; the expressive silent icon of the Blessed Virgin, and an Italian wedding scene beautiful enough to cause me to become Catholic (again).

This film portrays the frailty of life and the beauty of restoration. It is a relentlessly hopeful story that women of both sexes will enjoy. In my opinion the guys should bring the chocolate and peanut butter—and leave your Man-card at the door.

Fleeing Phil Dunphy

> Modern wisdom warns against hope. Modern
> parents caution their children, "Don't get your
> hopes up." We judge of man's wisdom by his
> hope. ~ Ralph Waldo Emerson

It's an established fact: parents do not live in reality.
Phil Dunphy, from the popular TV sitcom *Modern
Family*, is the quintessential example of 21st Century
American fatherhood. He is the Everyman of fathers.

When I was a 4-foot, 11-inch freshman in high school
(you heard me), my Dad regularly told me I was a
tough guy—tough enough to beat up "anyone in the
school." I knew what he was up to. He wanted me to
believe in myself. He wanted me to approach life from
a posture of confidence, yet he obviously didn't live in
my world. He had good intentions, but no wisdom to
help me through high school.

This is true of all parents. When my oldest daughter
went through high school she had a highly calibrated
sense of social judgment and hierarchy. She knew from
day to day who was "in" and who was "out." Check
that—she knew it from hour to hour. This time I was
the father: "*Honey, who cares what other people think?
You are smart, funny, warm, and beautiful.*" Right,
Dad.

I was disconnected from her world. I didn't know the
score, and what's more, I was powerless to change the
score. All the areas that matter to a teenage girl were

beyond what little influence or power I possessed. What's more, I suspect she would have been embarrassed if I really did know and understand her world. It belonged to her, not me.

The two lessons we learn growing up? Our loved ones may not have the wisdom or the power to help us. We are utterly on our own. Sometimes the best advice from our loved ones cannot provide the wisdom and strength we need to face our challenges. Experience teaches us that even if we trust our parent's heart and motives toward us, they do not have the wisdom to guide us, or the power to act on our behalf. We love them and they love us, but it is not enough.

This is precisely the heart of the problem: first-hand we see our parent's limitations, which means our experience also teaches us not to trust the Heavenly Father. One of the deepest transitions following our born-again experience is the need to grow up again—this time with the perfect parent. Paul wasn't kidding when he said:

> *So from now on we regard no one from a worldly point of view. Though we once regarded Christ in this way, we do so no longer. Therefore, if anyone is in Christ, the new creation has come: The old has gone, the new is here! (2 Corin 5:16-17)*

When he urged us not to regard anyone from a worldly point of view, it's important to include the Heavenly Father in that mix. We enter a new world, with a new Father, and the defenses we built up to protect us from our earthly parents can actually hold us back from the love and yes, power, that flows from the New Father. In God's kingdom, the Father displays perfect love (motivation), perfect wisdom (insight), and perfect power (strength to help us) toward his children.

After we come to terms with the idea that the One who knows us best loves us most, we have a second transformation: total surrender to the Perfect Father. We have so many years of disappointment; too many memories of our loved ones letting us down. Life experience has caused us to turn inward. We take care not to let our hearts fall too deeply in love. We live by the whispered caution, *"Take care: no one understands!"*

The good news is better than you could have ever hoped for. We have Father poised toward us with perfect love, wisdom, and power. In the Kingdom of God there is a new, established fact: our New Father see things the way they really are. We can trust him.

The People Magazine Spiritual Celebrity Index

> Hope is the feeling you have that the feeling
> you have isn't permanent. ~ Jean Kerr

Who can resist *People* magazine? It's the sugary donut of the mind. There you are, in the checkout line at the grocery store, and if you've successfully avoided *Cosmo* or the *National Inquirer, People* seems like a safe choice. Where else can you learn that Jennifer Lopez is the *Most Beautiful Woman in the World* and Bradley Cooper is *The Sexiest Man Alive*—but wait! That is *so* 2011. Six years later apparently both celebrities are no longer world-class beautiful.

And this is the spiritual application: I'm well aware of Jennifer Lopez and Bradley Cooper. I know more about them than I probably should, and I know less of Heaven's beauty than I should.

So, back in 2011 I developed a new way to take my spiritual temperature. I call it the *People Magazine Spiritual-Celebrity Index.* It works like this. There's a connection between my ability to recognize celebrities and my ability to recognize what the Kingdom of God values— it's an inverse relationship. These days I pick up People Magazine and look at the pictures, carefully avoiding the captions, and try to name the celeb. If I know them instantly, that's one negative point. If I think, "who is that?" that's one positive point. These days, for me, any score above zero is a winning score.

In fact, when I look at the magazines carefully, I see beauty in a dreary sameness: impossibly white teeth, complexions as smooth as ink on paper, and perfectly Photoshopped bodies. I'm beginning to understand what Leo Tolstoy said about happy families: "All happy families are alike; each unhappy family is unhappy in its own way." The same is true for modern beauty. How many astonishingly beautiful people do I need to see? But it's like drinking seawater—ten minutes later I'm thirsty for more beautiful sameness. This is what I value: a beauty that changes nothing in me, and cannot satisfy my soul.

When I turn to the letter of James (that's near the back of the New Testament), I discover a stern warning: "don't you know that friendship with the world means enmity against God? Therefore, anyone who chooses to be a friend of the world becomes an enemy of God." But James was always a buzzkill. Except he got his ideas from his big brother, Jesus, who said, "what is exalted among men is an abomination in the sight of God." Of course, James was talking about covetousness and Jesus was talking about money, but how difficult is it to make the connection to nearly everything we value in our society?

We need not reject society, nor do we need to criticize the values of this age. But we desperately need to refine our own tastes, and model the true beauty of God. We can all be cover girls of the Kingdom.

Here is the hope of beauty, a beauty that does not fade and cannot be marred: Heaven is filled with beauty, a beauty ethereal, eternal, and true. No doubt it dazzles the eye as well. But it is the fresh beauty of deep-down things, causing us to behold and become; giving us the freedom to admire without the desire to possess or use.

I want to gaze on the kind of beauty capable of changing me, carrying me from *glory to glory*, as Paul's graceful phrase reveals. What if Heaven's beauty is part of God's message, calling me upward and away from the passing pleasures (and tastes) of this present age. There is a lasting beauty, and it is beautiful because it invites me into a beautiful realm.

There's only one kind of beauty that transforms, and I won't find it online or at the checkout line.

Reflection #4

Here is the garden:
Hope is the seed
Cultivation is our task
Growth is the miracle beyond ourselves.

No matter our efforts, some things require miracles. But miracles are not as rare was we might suppose, nor do they happen randomly.

Jesus tells the short story of a farmer who sows the seed without any understanding of how things grow—but the farmer knows that things *do* grow! (Check it out: Mark 4:26-30) The farmer is no scientist, nor a theologian, but he has learned from experience that it is the nature of seeds to grow. So he does what he knows to do: till the soil, sow, the seed, and make ready for harvest time. The farmer didn't cause the seed to grow; yet he makes his living off the fact that the seed *does* grow!

So it is with hope.

Here is another meditation: what has your experience taught you about hope? Without understanding the why of hope, can you reflect on when your hopes have been fulfilled in the past? How did you "sow" it? How did you cultivate it? Take a moment and learn from your own experience and you'll discover that God provides the miracles, but miracles are a part of the fixed order of the earth.

Crackpots

If only for this life we have hope in Christ, we
are of all people most to be pitied.

~ 1 Corinthian 15:19

Walk among the tombstones in any cemetery and
you'll see signs of the sure and certain hope of
resurrection. Apart from Jesus, the grave is a place of
grief and finality. But, to borrow Michael Card's neat
phrase, in Jesus the grave became a place of hope.

Our Lord had a way of turning things around. The
cross, that Roman instrument of terror, became the sign
of love without borders. The cross was built to bend
others into submission; in Jesus the sign of the cross is
an invitation to a kingdom filled with righteousness,
peace, and joy.

One sure mark that "Jesus was here" is where the
signposts of despair are set on their heads and become
the evidence of his presence.

Nor is the mark of Jesus consigned to history: in Jesus,
his people gather the sick to hospitals where we will
pray for them, and if we cannot see them healed we
will care for them. If our care is not good enough we
will remain with them, because no one should die
alone. We make a place for the orphan; the very ones
cast aside by fate or the corrupted values of society
become the objects of our affection and treasure. We
go into the streets to find the homeless and hungry,
and—even if they have no interest in our gospel—we

give them food and warmth day after day in the hope that one day the message will take root.

All the while we ourselves are a disordered people, in need of these very ministries and more. We, who bear the good news, struggle to believe that anything this wonderful applies to us as well. Sometime God's people will share news so good we dare not believe it ourselves. This means we ourselves are markers of the kingdom: flawed, broken, incapable, and often ridiculous, we are the vessels of unspeakable grace. We are the cracked pots who carry and leak the eternal treasure poured out from heaven.

This is why I love His church, because even as we carve hope into tombstones, we ourselves are marked for death. Though we work in places of healing, we ourselves are subject to sickness. Even as we open our homes to others, we ourselves struggle with feelings of alienation. Who else would choose to use so mixed and fragile a collection of misfits? Only him who delights in turning refuse into treasure.

We ourselves are the markers of God's kingdom who declare, "we have absorbed the worst the world and the devil have to give, and in Jesus, we have seen darkness give way to dawn."

When Hope Comes Awake

Hope releases us from the bondage of time. We live in time, but hope takes us beyond time into all eternity. ~ Derek Prince

There's a kind of hope we cannot see without God's help. He must open our eyes to the possibilities of hope.

Opening our eyes to this hope is a bit like waking up, the kind of waking when, on our own, we simply realize we are now awake. In the quiet of the morning we find that sleep has gone. It's left us alone the bed. Then the thought occurs to us, "I'm awake . . . " We gently open our eyes and discover the room around us. Perhaps there is just enough light to see the familiar walls: the same room where, night-by-night, we lay ourselves to rest; the nightstand by the bed and the clothes we tossed on the chair last night; the familiar outlines of our bedroom, where we live out the rhythm of the days in all their sameness.

Right there, in that same room, that same house, with our same job and the same situation, in the moment of waking, there is always one thing new: it is a new day. It's exactly here that we need the Father to kiss our eyes awake so we can realize that although our world may be the same, this day is new. New morning; new mercies. This is the hope we cannot see without his help. Hope is the dawn before the fullness of the day.

The apostle Paul prayed on behalf of his friends in Ephesus: that they would awaken to this kind of hope.

I pray that the eyes of your heart may be enlightened, so that you will know what is the hope of His calling, what are the riches of the glory of His inheritance in the saints. (Ephesians 1:18)

Surely his prayer was inspired. Do you hear it? He prays that *the eyes of our heart will be enlightened,* asking that we would be given a kind of second sight, the kind that would allow us to *know the hope of his calling*—and a wonderfully strange calling it is—that we would awaken to the realization of what inheritance the Father has in us, his "saints." The "hope of His calling" in this prayer is the calling to see the richness of God in those around us! It would be foolish to limit our understanding of "God's calling" to some set of tasks the Almighty gives us to do (as if he is only a Taskmaster, demanding our service). No: God is calling us to see *the riches of his glory,* which we can discover in other people. Why should this come as a surprise? After all, we believe that all humanity is made in the image of God.

Hope is the realization that we are all saints (*holy ones*) because we are all set apart by the love of God. This kind of hope—which is only made possible by God's empowerment—awakens us to the fact that the Father has hidden something of himself in our brothers and sisters, those flawed saints we greet each day. In some sort of divine scavenger hunt he calls us to discover his presence in others. This is the kind of hope designed to empower us to see others as the Father sees them.

The hope of my calling includes the possibility to walk in the love of God, to see each woman and man as the Creator sees them. The hope of my calling is an invitation to imitate God by seeing people through God's eyes. And what peace becomes possible in this

114

invitation! This kind of hope has the potential to quiet the voice of judgment in my head, to reorder my affections for others, and to make me an instrument of God's peace. We have seen this kind of hope in operation through the life of Jesus—and through his followers. This kind of hope is at the heart of our calling. And finally, I do not need to accomplish this kind of calling on my own. I'm held steady by the hope of my calling: that walking in union with God is the Father's will, the Son's example, and the Spirit's promise.

Hope Incognito

To love means loving the unlovable. To forgive
means pardoning the unpardonable. Faith
means believing the unbelievable. Hope means
hoping when everything seems hopeless.

~ G.K. Chesterton

I caught up with Jesus one day a couple of years ago.
He was hanging out in a dingy hospital room in
Columbia, Kentucky.

His diabetes was acting up again, which was no
surprise because dumpster-divers don't have the best
diet even on a good day. He had already lost a few toes
here or there in the previous years, but this time he was
facing the possible loss of his foot. (Spoiler alert: don't
worry—I prayed for him, his condition improved, and
he ambled away from the hospital on both feet a few
days later.)

I'd actually been hanging out with Jesus for a couple of
months, but I'm a little slow to recognize old friends.

It started when a guy named Bill came to church. You
couldn't miss him: a rumple of a man well over six foot
tall, with shaggy wrinkled clothes topped off by a white
beard and white hair, neither of which had seen a
comb in weeks. Everything about him screamed
homeless. Bill's massive frame ambled along slowly as
the result of his missing toes. The only thing more
worrisome than whether he would make it to the coffee

bar without falling was the possibly that he *would* make it to the coffee bar and then try to walk away holding his hot coffee.

Bill and his coffee made it safely to one of our café-style tables, so I introduced myself. I did so more out of a concern for other's safety than to make him feel welcome. (When you see people like Bill your first thoughts are about the possibilities of what could go wrong.) I wanted to check him out first-hand. Everything about Bill was confusing. Where are you from? *I used to drive a truck in the Northeast.* How'd you hear about our church? *I drove by the other day.* Tell me about your family: *I think they're in Indiana, at least, they were the last time I talked to them.* When the service started Bill worshipped the same way most of us did, except he was taller, shabbier, and scarier than the rest of us. He raised his hands and tilted his head upward, soaking in the genuine praise around him.

Bill became a regular among us. He introduced us to the people in his entourage. He took care of Roberta, 60-plus years old: short, loud, and extremely off-putting. Plus, she was pretty ugly. One week Bill pulled me aside and apologized for her behavior and explained that her family had thrown her out on the street. He said he was now her only protection. They lived together in an abandoned mobile home out in the county. There didn't seem to be anything awkward about the arrangement because Roberta definitely needed protection, mostly from herself. A few weeks later Bill brought Doug and Maria, a thirty-something couple. Doug seemed almost normal and Maria was almost certainly mentally handicapped. They were both embarrassingly overweight. Bill told me they were down on their luck and needed a place to stay until they got up on their feet. Bill's squatter mobile home didn't have heat or electricity but it was safe and dry, so he opened his home to them.

Bill came to church early and loved to greet people. If they asked what he did for a living he smiled and said simply, "I'm a dumpster-diver." Which was true—that's how Bill cared for Roberta and provided shelter for Doug and Maria (although he once complained to me privately that Doug ate too much—especially the fresh produce he regularly scored at the supermarket dumpster.) The brave people who asked how Bill came into that line of work heard about the stroke he suffered while behind the wheel of a truck in downtown New York City. It seems Bill lost consciousness and drove the truck into the entrance of a Manhattan office building. That's when he switched careers.

One day Roberta came to church alone. She told me Bill was in the hospital.

Small-town Kentucky hospitals can be pretty depressing places, but when I walked into his room Bill looked up and gave me a smile from his bed. The smile was his big mistake; that's when I saw through his disguise and figured out I was in front of Jesus. I tried to play it cool and not let on. Bill asked about my family. He asked how the church was getting along. He put me completely at ease. There, in his hospital room, he was a gracious host.

The visit felt weird because I had come to pray for his foot. His circulation had failed. The foot was turning colors and he was likely to lose it above the ankle. He needed healing, but it's difficult praying over his ankle because after all, I was ministering to the Lord of Glory.

When we finished praying I asked him if he felt any better. He said, "I'm not worried. It'll all work out." It did. The circulation returned. He was discharged and came back to church just a few more times before he moved on to Indiana. He said he wanted to see his family.

A few months later I received a handwritten letter, blue ink on a notebook page. The ragged little pieces from where the page was torn out of the spiral notebook tickled the fingers of my left hand. Doug and Maria had found public-assisted housing. Roberta was ill and perhaps sick unto death. Bill was finding riches in the dumpsters of southern Indiana.

He thanked me for the welcome he had received in Kentucky. I sat holding the letter, but I couldn't recall if I had ever thanked *him*.

Made in the USA
Lexington, KY
19 December 2017